Text
Richard Coomber

Photography
Bruce Coleman Ltd.
Tom Hall

Design
Claire Leighton

Commissioning Editor
Andrew Preston

Commissioning Assistant
Edward Doling

Editorial
Jane Adams

Production
Ruth Arthur
Sally Connolly
David Proffit
Andrew Whitelaw

Director of Production
Gerald Hughes

Director of Publishing
David Gibbon

CLB 2557
© 1991 Colour Library Books Ltd., Godalming, Surrey, England.
This edition first published 1991 in Canada by B. Mitchell.
All rights reserved.
Printed and bound by Leefung Asco Printers Ltd, Hong Kong.
ISBN 0 88665 906 X

THE LIVING WORLD OF
CANADIAN BIRDS

RICHARD COOMBER

B. Mitchell

Introduction

From the Atlantic to the Pacific coast, and from the Arctic to the U.S. border, a mosaic of habitats provides breeding sites and feeding grounds for a great diversity of birdlife and many other forms of wildlife. Some species have a cosmopolitan distribution, but the majority only breed in North America. Some habitats and their inhabitants are not easy to pigeonhole; forests and woodlands, for instance, can cover areas of many square miles, yet an area in suburbia with many mature trees in gardens could perhaps also be classed as woodland. However, the balance of birds would not be the same as in true woodland, for additional species not normally present are attracted to feeders in gardens during the winter months.

Some birds are resident, remaining in their local areas throughout the year, while others are migratory, only living in their breeding areas during the spring and summer months. This is a condition imposed by the northerly position of the country, some areas of which can be far from hospitable places for birds, when in the grip of winter.

The American Avocet utters an alarm-like 'kleep' when disturbed. This bird's preferred habitat is the shallow lakes and sloughs of the southern prairie provinces.

The Semipalmated Plover is so named because of the partial webbing between its toes. Breeding on areas of sand, shingle or gravel tundra, usually near water, the Semipalmated Plover makes its nest of a hollow scrape, which it lines with bits of shell and plant material, and in which it usually lays four eggs.

On the grassy tundra, a female Pectoral Sandpiper guards her two newly hatched chicks.

The female Evening Grosbeak is identified by its heavy, conical bill and greyish plumage, with a greenish-yellow nape and much white on its wings and tail. In the breeding season these birds inhabit mixed or coniferous woodland, but in winter they can easily be attracted to garden feeding stations by the provision of sunflower seeds. They are most often seen in flocks.

As the climate of the earth warmed toward the close of the last ice age, Canada and the other countries that ring the Arctic Ocean were recolonised by birds that had retreated to more southerly latitudes at the onset of the ice and snow. As southern Canada became once more acceptable to certain species, so it also became less suitable for others whose distributions contracted toward the higher latitudes.

Food plays an all-important role in the distribution of birds, as with all forms of wildlife. During the long winter months, the insects on which such species as flycatchers, swallows and warblers depend are almost non-existent in the northern latitudes. The solution is simple: to migrate to areas where the climate is amicable and warm enough to support the abundance of insects needed to sustain their tiny bodies. In this case, it involves these species migrating south to the United States, Central or even South America. So, as summer days shorten and the season changes to fall, these travellers prepare for their long journey. They store energy as reserves of body fat to enable them to reach their wintering grounds.

North American songbirds do not encounter some of the hazards faced by their European counterparts; one such hazard is the birds' wholesale slaughter by "hunters" waiting in southern Europe and other Mediterranean countries before the birds can cross the arid wastes of the Sahara. The Canadian birds that winter in South America reach their destinations either by a sea crossing or by passing over Central America. Their biggest problem is the increasing destruction of the region's great primary forests, which have been home to countless generations. Some species have a restricted wintering range and appear to be unable to adapt to the habitat changes that follow the loss of their traditional wintering sites. This, more than any other single factor, may be responsible for the declining numbers of North American Wood Warblers.

It is not only the insectivorous birds that migrate, for countless thousands of shore birds and wildfowl leave their northern haunts of lakes, rivers and sloughs before snow covers their feeding grounds and areas of open water become locked in the iron grip of frost and ice. Some, such as the Pectoral and the Buff-breasted Sandpiper reach Patagonia; the noble and endangered Whooping Crane flies down to Aransas on the Gulf Coast of Texas, and the Common Loon leaves its lonely lakes for the open waters of the coast. Wildfowl migrate in large numbers from the Arctic to wetlands, some falling to the guns of hunters as they fly along traditional flyways in the United States.

The Common Snipe is usually seen perching in the open, on its breeding ground. The male's spring display flight includes a dive that, by vibrating air through its fanned tail feathers, produces a characteristic 'who-who-who' sound.

Breeding in eastern Canada, the Red-shouldered Hawk is so named after the reddish patch of feathers on its 'shoulder'. Its darkish wings have strong, white barring, and the blackish tail has narrow, white bands, while its whitish underparts are closely barred with reddish orange. This hawk inhabits mixed woodland, and is often seen either soaring in circles or perching whilst watching for its prey of small birds, frogs, reptiles and rodents.

The greatest traveller is the Arctic Tern, which breeds inside the Arctic Circle and winters along the edge of the Antarctic pack ice. This life style ensures that it sees more daylight in any twelve-month period than any other form of life. The movements of other species are not quite so dramatic. The American Dipper, for example, breeds along swift-flowing mountain streams, but may move in winter to lower elevations, where conditions are not so harsh and it can feed in open water.

Changes and movements in the bird populations are not only the result of climatic changes but also of habitat changes, and those caused by the European settlers are probably as great as any since the ice age. In many places the face of the land has changed beyond all recognition. Native forests and grasslands have been replaced with those that are more commercially viable; woodlands have been felled, but not replaced, and the drainage of some areas has been "improved" for the benefit of agriculture but to the detriment of wildlife. With many forms of wildlife having specific habitat requirements, they are the losers when such changes take place.

In the late twentieth century we appear to be on the threshold of more climatic changes, changes seemingly of our own making and not part of any natural cycle. As far as the birds are concerned, these will bring about changes in distribution, some advantageous but others sadly less so. If global warming occurs as predicted, a northwards expansion in the breeding range of some species can be envisaged; they might also begin to breed at higher elevations in the Rockies. Conversely, others will decline along the southern borders and at the lower elevations of their range. Two other possibilities are that some birds rarely seen in Canada during the winter could become more regular visitors and, as the levels of the world's oceans rise, there may also be an increase in such habitats as coastal marshes. Only time will tell, but it is up to each and every one of us to slow down and minimize these changes before they become irreversible.

Arctic and the High Country

The Arctic and the Rocky Mountains are among the last great wilderness areas of the northern hemisphere. They are home to many species of birds during the brief summer months; birds that, to those of us who live in "civilized" areas, are only winter visitors.

Comparatively few birds are resident in the high latitudes and at altitude throughout the year, the best examples of those that are being the ptarmigan, members of the grouse family. There are three species of ptarmigan, and all are highly adapted to their harsh environment; a double layer of body feathers together with feathered legs and feet act as protection against the cold. All three species look somewhat similar, especially in winter when they are in their white camouflaged plumage. The White-tailed Ptarmigan, found only amongst the peaks and high meadows of the Rockies, is the smallest of the three species and the whitest, possessing, as its name suggests, a completely white tail. The tail feathers of the Rock and the Willow Ptarmigan are black, these being mainly birds that inhabit the Arctic tundra. The Rock Ptarmigan inhabits bleaker, rockier and more barren areas than its slightly larger relative the Willow Ptarmigan. All three species moult in the spring into a cryptically coloured breeding plumage; both winter and summer plumages evolved to outwit such ever-watchful predators as the Gyr Falcon and the Arctic Fox.

The Arctic is home to countless millions of birds during the brief summer months. Many feed on the vast numbers of insects and their larva that populate these high latitudes, others feed on the fresh new plant growth that sprouts after the snows of winter melt each spring. Other birds, such as the Rough-legged Hawk and the Snowy Owl, depend on the lemming populations. In good years, when their food supply is abundant, they are able to rear more than their usual brood of about five youngsters; the trade-off being that when times are hard and there are few lemmings, the birds may not even attempt to breed! Both these species wander widely during the winter.

Jaegers are piratical, gull-like sea birds, which also benefit from a good lemming year. All three species of jaeger – Long-tailed, Parasitic and Pomarine – breed in the Canadian Arctic and winter at sea, where many reach the southern oceans. The smallest of the trio is

Willow Ptarmigan, like all other ptarmigan, have very different summer and winter plumages. In winter both sexes are all white, apart from their tails, which acts as camouflage in the snow. In spring, they begin to change to their summer plumage; the male is identified by the bright red combs above its eyes and its reddish-brown coloration – only the wings remain white. The Willow Ptarmigan is common on tundra, where it prefers damp habitats containing willow and alder.

A winter-plumaged Willow Ptarmigan, well camouflaged against the snow. This camouflage is very important, as ptarmigan are often preyed upon by birds such as the Gyrfalcon, that rely on their sight to locate prey.

A Rough-legged Hawk scavenging on an animal carcass. These hawks often hover whilst hunting and usually feed on rodents.

the Long-tailed Jaeger, which is about the size of a small gull but has a 10in.(25cm) long tail! The elongated central tail feathers are so flexible that they undulate behind the flying bird. It breeds on the tundra and numbers fluctuate with the available food supply. They feed largely on small rodents and nestlings. In a good lemming year, which occurs on average every four years, the jaegers and other predators will have a good breeding season, provided the weather is kind. Although not directly involved with the population dynamics of lemmings, other species also benefit from a good lemming year, when the abundance of this small rodent ensures that there is more than enough food for all. With predators such as the jaegers and Arctic Foxes concentrating their efforts on the easily caught lemmings, the infant mortality rate is lower than usual among sandpipers, longspurs and other species.

Several species of gull occur in the Arctic; the largest are the Glaucous Gull, the Iceland Gull and Thayer's Gull, but it is three small species that keen bird watchers perhaps particularly associate with the Arctic. The Ivory Gull is pure white, like driven snow, while an adult Ross' Gull in its breeding plumage is one of the most beautiful members of its family. The plumage has a pink flush contrasting with the black neck collar and grey wings. The third small species is

A male Snowy Owl, member of a diurnal species that breeds in the Arctic tundra.

A female Snowy Owl, whose distinctive brown barring distinguishes it from the almost completely white male. In summer the Snowy Owl feeds on lemmings in the northern tundra, moving further south as winter approaches.

Wintering in southern Canada, the Lapland Longspur breeds in the Arctic tundra. In winter it can be seen in flocks with Snow Buntings and Horned Larks, feeding along the shoreline or on grain stubble in fields. Their ground nest, a cup made of grass and lined with hair and feathers, is well hidden by surrounding vegetation.

A very common wading bird, the Least Sandpiper is the region's smallest sandpiper and prefers salt marshes and muddy shores.

Breeding in the Arctic, the Snow Goose is a common migrant to parts of eastern Canada, where many thousands can be seen feeding on the marshes. Two colour phases occur in this bird: the white phase and the 'blue' phase, which actually has a brown back.

Sabine's Gull, a more conventional looking gull with a black hood and striking black and white triangular wing patches.

Many species of wildfowl breed in the Arctic and none are more aptly named than the Tundra Swan and the Snow Goose. The Tundra Swan breeds around the Arctic Ocean, is smaller than the rarer Trumpeter Swan that occurs farther south but is a considerably rarer bird than the Snow Goose. The adult Tundra Swan may be seen with a rusty-coloured head. This is the result of staining by iron, which is present in the sediment at the bottom of pools and is disturbed while the bird's head is submerged as it feeds on underwater vegetation. The Snow Goose breeds in large numbers in the Arctic, and these then cross the southern provinces in the fall en route to wintering grounds along the Atlantic and Gulf coasts of the United States. In the west, the Snow Goose winters from southern British Columbia to California, where it is joined by the rare Ross' Goose – a small version of the Snow Goose. This is another Arctic breeder which is only known in a few areas in Arctic Canada. Both species have a "blue" phase besides the regular black and white form, but in the Ross' Goose this is very rare. Other geese that breed in the Canadian Arctic are the small races of the ubiquitous Canada Goose; the Greater White-fronted, which breeds west of Hudson Bay; and the Brant, which is

found in higher latitudes. Yet another, the Emperor Goose, is a rare winter visitor to coastal British Columbia from breeding grounds in northeastern Siberia and northwestern Alaska. It is a grey goose with a white head, giving the impression of a particularly clean-looking blue Snow Goose. Ducks are found in great numbers; some, such as the Northern Pintail, also breed elsewhere in Canada, but others, including the Oldsquaw and the King Eider, are mainly Arctic birds during the summer only.

Shore birds breed in profusion in the Arctic – a host of plovers and sandpipers, including some that winter as far away as South America. Perhaps most striking are the American Golden- and Black-bellied plovers in their nuptial plumage. The American Golden-Plover, recently split from its Asiatic counterpart, has a black face and underparts with spangled golden and black upper parts. The Black-bellied Plover is slightly larger with white and black spangling. Both species adopt an unassuming non-breeding plumage. The sandpipers make up those flocks of confusing "peeps" of muddy shores at migration times, but the other species that breed include the Hudsonian Godwit and the Eskimo Curlew. The godwit has a very restricted range in the Canadian Arctic, but that of the Eskimo Curlew is even more restricted. Eskimo Curlews formerly occurred in countless numbers, but were ruthlessly hunted by

The handsome King Eider is found mainly in the far north, and is rarely seen inland, spending most of its time around coastal waters, or on lakes and streams near the coast. It nests in the tundra, usually near fresh water.

The American Golden Plover is a bird of grassy plains, beaches and tundra. It is often seen in large flocks on migration. In spring, the species can be identified by its black face and underparts, its gold and black back and the striking white stripe that runs from its forehead to its upper breast.

man as they fed in huge migrating flocks in Labrador in the fall. The breeding range was never fully understood, and it now appears that the few pairs that may still exist probably breed in the Northwest Territories. In spring, instead of migrating along coastal areas, the remnant population migrates through the interior of Canada. The Eskimo Curlew is now so rare that it is not recorded annually, so that it is well worth double-checking the identity of any small whimbrel/curlew type during the spring passage. The Whimbrel, another Arctic shore bird, is far more plentiful and only differs from the Eskimo Curlew in its larger size, longer and more curved bill and lack of cinnamon colouring under the wing linings.

Two distinctive shore birds of the Arctic are the Red and Red-necked phalaropes, both smaller than Wilson's Phalarope, which is found in the freshwater marshes farther south. During the breeding season the Red occurs farther north than the Red-necked, which was formerly known as the Northern. Phalaropes differ from regular shore birds in that they habitually swim and delicately pick insects off the surface of the water while spinning like a top. Phalaropes are polyandrous, which means that the female is brightly coloured and seduces the male; when she has laid a clutch of eggs, she leaves him to get on with the incubation and subsequent rearing of

the chicks! Phalaropes are migrants and pass the winter at sea off the coasts of southern Africa and South America.

The Northern Wheatear is a summer visitor to the Arctic from the Old World. It is possible that this relative of the thrushes is a comparatively recent colonist of Canada, for birds still migrate through western Europe to winter in Africa – a long way from Canada. The name "wheatear" comes from the Anglo-Saxon "white arse," a reference to the distinctive white rump the bird displays when in flight.

Arctic songbirds, or passerines, include the Lapland Longspur, Smith's Longspur, and the Snow Bunting. Once stunted willows and birch enter the landscape, so the Common Redpoll, the Hoary Redpoll, and a few warblers, juncos and sparrows are added to the list, which further increases as one enters the boreal forests.

Heading south, an Arctic-like habitat is found above the tree line in the Rocky Mountains. This bare and sometimes rocky habitat is home to relatively few resident species; the White-tailed Ptarmigan mentioned earlier and the Common Raven are two of the larger resident species. The Common Raven is found in a variety of "wilderness" habitats ranging from the Arctic to Central America. This bird has learned to take advantage of man's garbage tips. The Golden Eagle is another inhabitant of the high country

An adult male Hudsonian Godwit. This bird is mainly a migrant to Canada; although it does nest in parts of the country, much of its breeding range is unknown. In flight its white wing stripes, black tail and white rump are striking; it is also identified by its slightly upcurved bill.

One distinctive feature of the Golden Eagle is the yellow, fleshy cere at the base of the bill. The bill itself is nearly as long as the bird's head.

A Golden Eagle with its marmot prey. The eagle's favourite hunting grounds are foothills with grassy pastures where prey such as the yellow-bellied marmot live.

that also is found in remote places. Although the Golden Eagle may scavenge like the Bald Eagle, it is an accomplished hunter of hare, marmot and ptarmigan.

In the mountains of northwestern Canada the Surfbird and the Wandering Tattler breed; both these birds are winter visitors to the rocky Pacific coasts. In summer the Surfbird is to be found on the alpine heaths above the tree line, while the Tattler is associated with the gravel beds of swift-flowing mountain streams. At these altitudes their neighbours include the Common Raven, the Water Pipit and the Rosy Finch.

To go north and see birds on their breeding grounds, with the males in full nuptial dress, is always an exciting experience.

The Golden Eagle is distinguished by its strong, hooked beak, overall brown plumage and feathered legs.

Far left: a Gyrfalcon with its prey. This falcon feeds mainly on large birds, such as ptarmigan, and rodents, and it occurs in three colour phases: a grey phase; a dark phase, which is brown, and a white phase, which is the commonest in the stern high Arctic. The Great Horned Owl (left and below left) is Canada's biggest owl and takes prey as large as hares.

The Hawk Owl has a long tail, which gives it a falcon-like appearance, especially in flight. Other distinguishing features are its heavily-barred underparts and the black border of its pale facial disk. A diurnal owl, it is often seen prominently perched on a tree top, where it has the curious habit of flicking its tail up and then lowering it slowly. Its flight is rapid, interspersed with glides, and it also hovers. This owl inhabits the muskegs and coniferous and deciduous woodland of northern Canada, and is usually very tame.

Once known as the Pigeon Hawk, the Merlin is a very small, dashing falcon. In flight it shows considerable bursts of speed as it chases its prey, which consists of small birds. A strongly-barred tail and pointed wings help its identification.

A handsome Pacific Loon, resplendent in its summer plumage. This loon breeds on freshwater lakes in the remote north and winters on the coast.

The Whistling Swan (right), a magnificent, all-white bird, breeds in the Canadian low Arctic. The Common Redpoll (far right) is identified by its streaked plumage, short stubby bill, red cap and black chin; the breast of the male is usually tinged with pink. In winter this bird is often seen feeding on the seeds of alder and birch trees.

Coniferous Forests and Deciduous Woodland

In a country rich in timber, it is hardly surprising to find there are many birds that breed exclusively in the vast stretches of coniferous forests and deciduous woodlands. Some birds that are associated with these habitats have also become familiar garden species. They find that the shrubs and trees we plant, together with the relative security afforded by gardens (barring cats of course!), constitute an acceptable substitute for the understorey and secondary growth of woodland. Other species stay loyal to their ancestral homes during the breeding season, but may visit gardens if food is provided for them during the winter months.

The great coniferous forests are home to two large species of grouse. The Blue and the Spruce Grouse are closely related, but during display the male Blue Grouse inflates a yellow or red neck patch surrounded by a ring of white feathers. This species ranges from the Rockies westwards, while the slightly smaller Spruce Grouse occurs across the breadth of mainland Canada; it was also introduced to Newfoundland. Another forest ground dweller, but one found in mixed and secondary woodland, is the Ruffed Grouse. It has roughly the same distribution as the Spruce Grouse but was also successfully introduced into a different habitat in Newfoundland.

The Wild Turkey also inhabited the forests of southern Canada, but became extinct through habitat destruction and possibly overhunting around the turn of the century. Since then there have been various attempts to reintroduce this fine bird back into the wild, but these have met with little success, one notable exception being a 1962 introduction to southeastern Alberta, from which birds have now spread into neighboring Saskatchewan.

The forests are the haunt of three bird-hunting hawks. The Northern Goshawk is about the size of a buteo, while the Sharp-shinned Hawk is similar in size to an American Kestrel; the third member of the trio, Cooper's Hawk, falls between the two. They are long-tailed raptors with short, broad wings; the Northern Goshawk and the Sharp-shinned Hawk have the wider distribution while Cooper's Hawk is limited to a band across the southern provinces.

The Spruce Grouse inhabits coniferous forests the width of Canada and, being very tame, will allow the approach of humans.

With red combs erect, cocked tail spread and throat puffed out, the male Spruce Grouse beats his wings in courtship display.

Fanning its broad, rounded tail, the male Ruffed Grouse tries to attract a female. The black feathers on the side of the neck, which form a ruff, distinguish this bird from all other grouse. It has two colour phases: grey and, in the southwest, red, though the colour variations usually relate only to the tail colour.

The Ruffed Grouse inhabits mixed woodland, especially the clearings within woods, and can be found in a wide area west to east across Canada.

The Wild Turkey was once extinct in Canada, but successful attempts have now been made to reintroduce it into hardwood forests, where it feeds on acorns, fruit and seeds.

The male Wild Turkey demonstrating his elaborate courtship display.

With its short, rounded wings and long tail, the Northern Goshawk is ideally suited to chasing and catching prey in woodland. Flying through the trees at low level, it can then swoop on its prey, such as squirrels and grouse. This hawk's long, yellow legs and its feet with their large, needle-sharp claws are ideal for clasping and gripping prey.

The adult Northern Goshawk is identified by the greyish barring on its underparts and the white line above its eye. The goshawk's nest is constructed almost entirely by the male, and the hawk breeds in woodlands throughout most of central and southern Canada.

Other raptors present in woodlands are the buteos the most widespread of which is the Red-tailed Hawk, a bird related to the Common Buzzard of the Old World. Both enjoy similar habitats, both hover into the wind and both have learned to utilize telegraph poles as lookout posts. In winter, Red-tailed Hawks withdraw from the northern part of their range and, although some winter in the southern provinces, the majority head farther south. In North America a "buzzard" is a Turkey Vulture. The whole of the Broad-winged Hawk population, which breeds across southern Canada east of British Columbia, also leaves in winter, when it can be found from Mexico to Brazil. Another member of the family is the Red-shouldered Hawk, which has a limited distribution in southeastern Canada and also moves south in the fall.

Owls seem to hold a particular fascination for people in general, and for birders in particular. Canada is fortunate in having sixteen breeding species, the majority being birds of the forests and woodlands. Some, including the Northern Pygmy-Owl, the Boreal Owl and the Great Gray Owl, are birds of the northern and montane coniferous forests and of these it is the enigmatic Great Gray Owl that many birders hold in high esteem. It is the largest of the North American owls and has a disproportionately large head. With its long tail and the hawk-like flight that gives it its name, the Northern Hawk-Owl is

When fully mature, Cooper's Hawk is identified by the reddish barring on its underparts and by its long, rounded tail. Immature birds have pale underparts with fine, dark streaking. An uncommon hawk, it inhabits woodland across the southernmost parts of Canada.

The Broad-winged Hawk is one of the smaller hawks, and is found mainly in woodland. It usually hunts alone and from a perch, where it waits for prey such as snakes, frogs or mice to pass below; on the other hand, large numbers of these hawks can be seen congregating for migration in the autumn.

The Long-eared Owl is readily identified by its distinctive ear tufts. Locally common, it breeds in both deciduous and coniferous woodlands.

another owl from the northern forests that may reach southern Canada, and beyond, during its winter wanderings. The Spotted Owl is one of the rarest North American Owls and in Canada it is confined to the coniferous forests of southwestern British Columbia. Its rarity has brought conservationists and foresters into direct confrontation in the U.S. over logging and the destruction of the owl's preferred habitat of dense mature forests. The Barred Owl, a close relative of the Spotted Owl, and the Long-eared Owl have a wider range and breed in both deciduous and coniferous woodlands. The other large owl with "ears" is the Great Horned Owl, the most widespread owl in Canada. It lives in a variety of woodland habitats, although sometimes it is a bird of more open areas, nesting on cliff ledges if trees are not available. The smallest of the Canadian "eared" owls are the screech owls; formerly one species, the experts now call those in British Columbia the Western Screech Owls and those east of the Rocky Mountains the Eastern Screech Owls. The precise dividing line between the two is not clearly understood.

The forests can claim few shore birds; one name that springs to mind of course is the American Woodcock, a cryptically coloured bird related to the snipe of the marshes and possessing a distinctive steep forehead and broad, rounded wings. It inhabits a variety of woodland types in eastern Canada. One

The tiny, tuftless Saw-whet Owl prefers to nest in moist, mixed forest and, although commoner than is generally thought, is rarely seen because of its nocturnal habits.

The Great Horned Owl is often woken and mobbed by crows during the day. Identifiable by its large size and conspicuous ear tufts, this particular owl inhabits deciduous and coniferous woodland, city parks and river valleys, where it hunts rabbits, skunks, ducks and grouse, as well as rats and mice. Its call is a loud, deep hoot, usually uttered three to five times.

A Barred Owl emerges
from its nest site in a
hollow tree; this species
usually nests in cavities.

A female American
Woodcock and its chick
sit tight on their nest,
perfectly camouflaged
amongst the dead leaves
of the forest floor.

does not usually think of shore birds as tree-nesting species, but the Solitary Sandpiper of the northern forests uses the old nests of other birds: these often include the American Robin, the Gray Jay and those passerines that make a large enough cup-shaped nest. The Solitary Sandpiper is closely related to the Green Sandpiper of the Old World, which also uses old nests and occupies a similar ecological niche.

When Canada was first settled by Europeans, there was a pigeon whose numbers ran into millions in southern Canada and the northern United States, and whose colonies were measured in square miles! These birds migrated annually to winter in the southeastern United States and, as agriculture expanded, so the Passenger Pigeon and man came into head-on conflict. War was declared; colonies were destroyed en masse, so that the last reliable

The Grey Jay inhabits the northern forests, where it is locally common, even becoming tame around lumber camps.

The female Rufous Hummingbird; this species can be found breeding in parts of western Canada.

The male Rufous Hummingbird displaying the unmistakable colouring that gives the species its name.

The Calliope Hummingbird is not only the smallest Canadian hummingbird, it is also the smallest North American bird of any kind. Its nest is minute, less than an inch high, and is bound together with spiders' webs.

Found exclusively in southwest Canada, Lewis' Woodpecker inhabits open woodland. It differs from most other woodpeckers not only in having a steady, undulating flight of slow wingbeats, but also in catching most of its insect food in the air. Its red face, grey breast and collar, pink belly and greenish-black head and back give it a distinctive, easily identifiable appearance.

Yellow-bellied Sapsuckers, like all sapsuckers, are so named for their habit of drilling holes in trees, which they later revisit to feed on both the sap and the various insects attracted to the sweet resin. These birds are common in deciduous woodland.

Canadian sighting was in 1902 and the species became extinct in 1914 when the last individual, Martha, died at Cincinnati Zoo. Nowadays the most widespread member of the family is the Mourning Dove, a familiar bird of open woodland, urban and agricultural areas all across the southern provinces. In British Columbia, the Band-tailed Pigeon reaches the northern end of its range along the Pacific coastal belt.

From the Rockies to Newfoundland, open woodland and thickets are the haunt of the Black-billed Cuckoo, while the similar Yellow-billed Cuckoo is confined to the southeastern corner of the country. Cuckoos are migrants from wintering areas in South America. The nightjars are also migrants; they are cryptically coloured birds of wooded habitats and include the Common Nighthawk, Poorwill, Chuck-will's-widow and Whip-poor-will. These birds are mainly active from dusk onwards, when the feed on moths and other nocturnal insects. They are helped in this by their large eyes and broad mouths, which are surrounded by sensitive bristles that help them to detect their prey in the dark. Sometimes the Common Nighthawk can be seen hunting during the day.

Some of the most aerial of birds are the swifts, who eat, sleep and even mate on the wing. Before houses with chimneys appeared on the scene, the Chimney Swift bred in hollow trees, and being summer migrants, they found that dormant chimneys were equally acceptable! The bird breeds from Saskatchewan eastward. In the west, Vaux's Swift also uses hollow trees, and less frequently chimneys. The Black and the White-throated swifts, the only other Canadian representatives of the family, breed at sites in cliffs and other rocky places.

Hummingbirds reach the northern limits of their range in Canada with the most widespread of the five breeding species being the Ruby-throated Hummingbird. This is the common eastern species and is usually the only one to breed east of the Rockies. In the conifers of the Rockies the Calliope and Rufous hummingbirds occur, the latter ranging west to the Pacific coast. Recently both the Black-chinned and Anna's hummingbirds have extended their ranges northward from the United States to establish a tenuous foothold in British Columbia. Naturally all hummers migrate south in the fall.

The woods and forests provide food and nest sites for fourteen species of Canadian woodpecker, but to maintain this variety there are distinct habitat preferences among species. Lewis' Woodpecker inhabits scattered trees in open country, while the Black-backed and closely related Three-toed woodpeckers are birds of the coniferous forests of the mountains and the north. Together with four other species, they occur across the country; this group

also includes the smallest of the species – the tiny Downy Woodpecker – and the largest – the striking Pileated Woodpecker. Most species are resident, the exception being the sapsuckers. The western form of the widespread Yellow-bellied Sapsucker, known as the Red-naped Sapsucker, has recently been given specific status; both winter from the southern United States to Central America and the Caribbean. Williamson's Sapsucker retreats into the United States, while the Red-breasted Sapsucker is limited to southwestern British Columbia in the winter months. The name "sapsucker" is quite a mouthful, especially when preceded by a double-barrelled name, but these birds do indeed suck sap! Another recent taxonomic change has been the "lumping together" of the Red-shafted and Yellow-shafted flickers to form just one species – the Northern Flicker.

Wooded habitats across Canada are home to many songbirds – those passerines that have highly developed vocal organs and, usually, a musical call. Many, the Wood Warblers for example, are summer visitors from wintering areas in the United States, the Caribbean, and Central and South America. One look at a well illustrated field guide shows page after page

An Ovenbird feeds its young, safe in the domed nest built by the female among the deep leaf litter on the floor of deciduous woodland – the bird is usually seen on the ground. A warbler, the Ovenbird is distinguished by its brownish-orange crown bordered by blackish stripes and its white eye ring.

A Hermit Thrush feeds its young in a nest built low down in a conifer. This bird is perhaps the finest songster in Canada, although its song is rarely heard outside its breeding ground.

of colourful male birds in the nuptial plumages that contrast with their plainer and more confusing non-breeding plumages. In the latter case, it is a matter of trying to distinguish wing bars and tail spots, for migrating birds are not necessarily faithful to their breeding habitats. During the breeding season, warblers are found in a variety of woodland habitats; the species involved include the Northern Parula, the Tennessee, the Black-and-white, the Cerulean, the Blackburnian, the Yellow-rumped, and the Black-throated Green warblers, as well as the Louisiana and Northern waterthrushes. In the coniferous forests are found such types as the Cape May, Magnolia, Bay-breasted, Blackpoll, Townsend's and Pine warblers while others, including the Black-throated Blue, Chestnut-sided, Black-throated Gray, Prairie, Canada, Prothonotary and Hooded warblers, the American Redstart, and the Ovenbird inhabit the deciduous woodlands. Another group, made up of the Orange-crowned, Nashville, Palm, Yellow, Mourning, MacGillivray's, Connecticut and Wilson's warblers, and the Common Yellowthroat, are found around woodland margins, in thickets, tangles and other secondary growth. The endangered Kirtland's Warbler formerly bred amongst immature jack pines in southern Ontario, but this species is declining and is now only breeding in Michigan. This decline appears irreversible, so with a population in the low hundreds

and a migration route that takes it out to the Bahamas, extinction seems inevitable. Vireos are similar to warblers, but appear slightly heavier in build. Of the seven species that breed in Canada, the Philadelphia, Red-eyed, Solitary and Warbling vireos are the most widespread. They are birds of deciduous or mixed woodland, summer visitors from the southern United States, Central or South America.

Old World warblers are represented in Canada by the kinglets and the Blue-gray Gnatcatcher. The Golden-crowned and Ruby-crowned kinglets are tiny birds of coniferous and mixed woodland, and they occur across the width of the country. The gnatcatcher reaches the northern limits of its range in the deciduous woodland and thickets of southern Ontario and Quebec.

These birds belong to the same group of passerines as the thrushes, whose best known representative is the American Robin – despite its name, not strictly speaking a true robin, but a thrush. The robin is a European species that is a familiar garden bird in Britain, where it is still known in non-ornithological circles as the "robin redbreast." Thus, whenever explorers discovered any new bird with a red breast, they inevitably called it a "robin." The American Robin is a bird of woods and marginal habitats, but by winter it has moved out from all but the extreme south to winter in the United States. In the woods and forests other members of the family spend the breeding season adding their songs to those of other summer visitors. The North American thrushes have brown upper parts and spotted or

The Mountain Bluebird nests in holes in trees, sometimes occupying abandoned woodpecker holes. A fairly common bird, it does, as its name implies, inhabit high country, although it winters at sea level.

streaked breasts; all five breed in Canada, with Swainson's and the Hermit thrushes being the most widespread. The Veery occurs across the southern provinces, while the Gray-cheeked Thrush is more northerly in its range. The Wood Thrush is expanding its distribution and now breeds from southern Ontario to Nova Scotia with an outpost in southern Manitoba.

Bluebirds are also relatives of the thrushes and need no introduction. The Eastern Bluebird occurs across eastern Canada from southern Saskatchewan to Nova Scotia. In the West the Mountain Bluebird ranges from Manitoba to the Alaskan border, far more extensive than the Western Bluebird which is limited to southern British Columbia.

The tropics of the Americas are home to the tyrant Flycatchers, a huge family of often closely-related species. Some reach the woods, forests and thickets of Canada for the breeding season. Olive-sided, Yellow-bellied, Alder and Least flycatchers occur in suitable habitats over much of the country south of Hudson Bay. Others are localized in either the east or the west but may have counterparts, such as the Eastern- and Western-Wood pewees, on opposite sides of the country. Others, including Hammond's and the Dusky flycatchers, are western in distribution, and recently the Western Flycatcher has been split into two species. Those of the Pacific coast are now Pacific-slope Flycatchers, while the Rocky Mountain

birds have become the Cordilleran Flycatchers. This does not make them any easier to identify in the field! A total of twenty-six species occur in Canada, but not all of them breed, for some, such as the Gray Kingbird, and the Scissor-tailed and Fork-tailed flycatchers, are accidentals from much farther south.

The Tree Swallow is a widespread member of the swallow family and breeds across Canada. It usually nests in old woodpecker holes or other tree cavities, a preference it shares with the beautiful Violet-green Swallow; their nesting sites range from the Pacific coast to the Rockies, although the latter also may use suitable crevices in cliffs. Like all the other northern members of the family, they are only summer visitors to the area. The Purple Martin also nests in holes in trees but can be attracted to strategically placed nestboxes.

The Brown Creeper and the nuthatches are also woodland birds which have developed a life style that involves climbing trees like woodpeckers. The Brown Creeper is a mouse-like, insectivorous bird of mature woodlands in the southern provinces, while the most widespread of the three nuthatch species is the Red-breasted Nuthatch. Nuthatches are named for their habit of opening nuts placed in a crack in the bark of a tree. They are more solidly built than the Brown Creeper and have a much stouter bill. The small Pygmy Nuthatch is confined to the western

A Red-breasted Nuthatch enters its nest hole bearing food for its young. This is the only Canadian nuthatch with a white stripe.

A Pygmy Nuthatch at the entrance to its nesting hole, which it has excavated in the dead wood of a tree. As its name suggests, this is the smallest nuthatch found in Canada, and it inhabits ponderosa woodland.

The Cedar Waxwing is so named because of the red, waxy tips to its wing feathers; it also boasts a fluffy crest and is often seen in large flocks.

Small and secretive, the Winter Wren lives in cavities; the nest is built by the male and lined by the female.

The conspicuous crest of the Blue Jay is one distinguishing mark of this colourful, year-round Canadian resident.

The adult Blue Jay tends to its young in their tree nest. Colourful birds, with blue upperparts and white underparts, these jays are easily identified by the white in their wings and tail, which distinguishes them from other blue-winged jays. Noisy and inquisitive, the Blue Jay can be found in woodlands, parks and suburban gardens.

mountainous forests, while the White-breasted Nuthatch occurs in several areas in southern Canada. In winter this species may visit garden feeders for peanuts, where it can be found alongside Black-capped Chickadees. Chickadees are small, busy woodland birds with a dark cap. The Black-capped and the Boreal chickadees are the most widespread; western forests contain the Chestnut-backed and Mountain chickadees, although the latter is more a bird of the mountainous forests, as its name suggests. In the northwest of the Northwest Territories, the Siberian Tit reaches the eastern limit of its range in the New World. Heading westward this bird ranges all the way round to Norway! In the east, the Tufted Titmouse is extending its range from the United States, where in winter it too benefits from the provision of garden feeders.

Wrens are another family of small birds some of which are found in woodlands and thickets. They are New World in origin with only the Winter Wren, the most widespread of the eight Canadian species, occurring in the Old World. The House Wren is a larger edition of the Winter Wren, but not as extensive in its range. Other wrens associated with this habitat are Bewick's and the Carolina, but both have only a foothold in the country. Of the four remaining Canadian species, the Marsh and Sedge wrens are birds found in marshland, while the Canyon and Rock

wrens are, as their names suggest, birds of open and rocky country.

Among the variety of other birds associated with woodlands in one form or another are the shrikes and the waxwings. Across the northern edge of the tree line lives the Northern Shrike, a predatory passerine with a hooked bill and the habit of impaling its prey on thorns to form larders – hence its alternative name of "Butcherbird." It is grey and white with a long tail and a distinctive black mask. The Loggerhead Shrike

Steller's Jay is found in western Canada; its dark crest is an obvious distinguishing mark.

A frequent visitor to gardens in the west, Steller's Jay can also be seen on campsites in mixed or coniferous woodland.

'Kra-a-a' is the call of Clark's Nutcracker, whose all-grey body contrasts with its black wings and tail; the outer tail feathers and a small wing patch are white. This nutcracker inhabits high, coniferous forests, often descending in winter to scavenge at campsites.

Clark's Nutcracker generally feeds on the nuts and conifer seeds that are common in its preferred coniferous habitats near the timberline.

Often found in flocks in winter, the Pine Grosbeak has the strong, heavy bill typical of a seed-eater. The males are a beautiful rose-red colour, with white wing bars that contrast with the otherwise dark wings.

The male Evening Grosbeak is a large, handsome and distinctively-plumaged finch, readily identified by its huge, whitish beak, yellow forehead that extends back behind and above the eye, yellow underparts and broad, white patch in an otherwise black wing. Grosbeaks breed throughout southern Canada, and are often seen in noisy flocks uttering a loud, house-sparrow-like chirp.

The Rose-breasted Grosbeak is common in deciduous woodland, where it is easily identified by its distinctive black head and back, white wing bars, massive bill and the bright red patch on its breast. In flight its red wing linings and the white patches on its wings are visible from below.

The Purple Finch is not as purple as its name suggests, but is rather rose red in colour. It breeds in open woodland across most parts of southern Canada, though it can also be seen in suburban gardens.

is slightly smaller and has a more southerly range. Waxwings are another pair of woodland birds, with the Bohemian Waxwing having a more northerly and western distribution than the smaller Cedar Waxwing. The latter occurs from Newfoundland to British Columbia in a variety of wooded habitats, whereas the Bohemian Waxwing is mainly a bird of coniferous woodland.

Crows are usually thought of as big and black, but this is not necessarily the case for jays, magpies and nutcrackers are also members of the Crow family. Across much of the country the Gray Jay inhabits a variety of woodland types, while the more familiar and colourful Blue Jay occurs south and east of the Rockies, with little overlap. In the west, the darker Steller's Jay has a more extensive range than Clark's Nutcracker, a striking grey and black bird that shows white wing patches in flight. In more open wooded country lives the Black-billed Magpie a notorious robber of other nests, and a species that occurs widely across Eurasia. Finally, to the black crows. The most widespread of these is the American Crow, which is familiar across the country, except along the Pacific coastal belt where it is replaced by the Northwestern Crow. The two are very similar and the field guides suggest that the best way of distinguishing between the two is by distribution. Last is the Common Raven, a bird whose range takes it through a variety of wilderness habitats from the Arctic through to Central America.

The coniferous forests are home to several species of seed-eating birds that only occur in other habitats when forced to do so by adverse weather conditions in winter. Largest of these birds is the Pine Grosbeak, a thrush-sized finch that usually winters within its breeding range. The male is a rose-coloured bird, while his mate is brown. Smaller, similarly coloured versions are Cassin's, House and Purple finches, although these females have striated underparts. Cassin's Finch is restricted to western forests; the Purple Finch ranges from Newfoundland to British Columbia and from the United States border to Hudson Bay, while until recently the House Finch was a strictly western bird. This began to change in 1940 when House Finches were released on Long Island, New York, where they became established as a breeding species. From here they spread outwards, helped by the convenience of garden feeders during the winter, and in 1978 the first breeding took place in southern Ontario, since when the House Finch has spread slowly north and east. The Red Crossbill and the White-winged Crossbill are specialist feeders with crossed mandibles that enable the birds to prise open pine cones to reach the seed inside. Another finch found in these forests is the Pine Siskin, which has a finer bill than other finches and so can extract seeds

Cassin's Finch is found only in a small area of southwest Canada, and is very similar to the Purple Finch. It can be distinguished from the former by its more distinctive capped appearance and its 'kee-up' call.

The extraordinary bill of the Red Crossbill is specially designed to extract the seeds from pine cones. The male is identified by its reddish plumage, the female being yellowish. Inhabiting coniferous woodlands, these birds are sometimes common, according to the availability of pine cones. Interestingly, young birds do not develop the crossed bill until some ten days after leaving the nest.

more simply.

Orioles are summer visitors to open deciduous woodlands. In Canada, the Northern Oriole occurs in the southern provinces where it is more widespread than the Orchard Oriole which is found along the border. Male orioles are striking black, yellow and orange birds, far brighter than some other members of the Icterid family to which they belong. Other members of the family are the blackbirds; some, such as the Yellow-headed and Red-winged blackbirds, breed in marshes, while Brewer's and the Rusty blackbirds, together with the Common Grackles, are birds of more wooded habitats. Outside the breeding season blackbirds may be found in open areas and can be an agricultural pest at times.

Woodland and forested habitats are hosts to many other species of seed- and insect-eating birds. There are grosbeaks with their large bills, redpolls, goldfinches, towhees and sparrows, but one in particular stands out – an immaculate male Western Tanager in his bright plumage of black, red and yellow. Surely a bird to inspire anyone to pick up a pair of binoculars and go birding!

Conspicuous yellow and white wing bars identify the Western Tanager, which is found in mixed or coniferous woodland in western Canada.

The adult male Western Tanager is distinguished from the female by its red head, both sexes having bright yellow underparts as well as the conspicuous double wing bars.

Two seven-week-old Bald Eagle chicks patiently await their parents' return with food. These birds will fly in another three to four weeks, but still may return to the nest for food. The nest itself, built in a tall tree, may become huge, as it is often returned to and enlarged year after year.

A Bald Eagle, bill agape, utters its squealing 'kik-kik-kik' call.

Freshwater Lakes, Rivers and Marshes

Canada's freshwater habitats come in all shapes and sizes, from the Great Lakes, which are almost inland seas, to small ponds surrounded by cattails; from swift mountain streams full of meltwater to slow meandering rivers brown with the silt washed from the land after periods of rain; and from sloughs, whose water levels change with the seasons, to the countless bogs and pools that appear in the tundra as the ice and snow of winter melt. The tundra wetlands, although freshwater, are an integral part of the Arctic ecosystem and for the purposes of this book are covered in that section.

It is in the large lakes across Canada that the Common Loon is to be found during the breeding

The Common Loon returns to its breeding grounds by lakes and rivers soon after the winter ice breaks up.

The Great Blue Heron, Canada's largest heron, is a statuesque bird that gives a harsh alarm call of four hoarse squawks.

As well as being Canada's largest heron, the Great Blue Heron is also the country's most numerous. It has a dramatic method of hunting; either standing motionless in the water or slowly stalking its prey – mainly fishes or amphibians – the heron will suddenly lunge forward and grasp the unfortunate victim in its bill.

The Great Blue Heron in flight.

The elegant stretch of the Great Blue Heron captured at takeoff.

season. This is the most widespread of the four members of its family to breed in Canada. The wonderful haunting cry of the loon echoing back from the tree-lined lakes is a sound that is part of the special atmosphere in the back country. Loons are fish-eating birds that catch their prey by diving from the surface of the water, hence the Old World name of "divers." The other three species, the Yellow-billed, Pacific and Red-throated loons, are essentially breeding birds of tundra lakes, yet in winter all four species may be found in coastal waters for they are equally at home amongst the waves. The Yellow-billed Loon, rarest of the three, and the Pacific Loon are found along the coast of British Columbia, while the other two occur along both the Atlantic and Pacific coasts.

Grebes are also freshwater fishermen, but are found in smaller areas of water where there are reeds and floating vegetation to provide suitable nesting sites. Their nests of waterweeds and other vegetable matter may be secured to living plants. Largest of these birds is the Western Grebe, an elegant bird with an elaborate courtship dance. To the east of the Rockies it breeds on lakes in central southern Canada, while to the west of the mountains it inhabits southern British Columbia. Later in the year the Western Grebe becomes a coastal species in British Columbia as birds move out from the interior before

the onset of winter. Recently the pale phase of the Western Grebe has been given specific status and is now known as Clark's Grebe, although its breeding range within Canada is not yet fully defined.

The dumpy Pied-billed Grebe inhabits lakes and ponds, often living near marginal vegetation. During the breeding season the bird's black and white bill is its most distinctive feature, and it is from this that the grebe earns its name. In winter the bill is plain white; similarly, in the autumn, the other grebes loose their colourful plumage in favour of plain grey, black and white garb. Thus, the Red-necked Grebe looses its red neck and the Eared and Horned grebes lose the orange and yellow plumes that give them their "ears" and "horns" respectively.

Herons and egrets are often conspicuous birds of freshwater wetlands, as personified by the stately Great Blue Heron, a master fisherman who stands patiently by pool or stream, ever watchful for an unsuspecting fish. When the victim comes into view, the bird tenses, moves slowly into striking range, then snatches the fish with a sudden stab, and holds it firmly between the upper and lower mandibles for a few brief moments before swallowing it whole. The Great Blue occurs over much of Canada east of the Rockies and south of the Great Lakes. It is absent from the Rockies and, in British Columbia, is mainly a bird of coastal areas and of islands such as Vancouver

A Green-backed Heron resting on a rock. This heron is seen along wooded streams or on small ponds more commonly than are other herons. At a distance it often appears to be all dark.

A Green-backed Heron with a successful catch of small fish in its bill. It often perches amid semi-submerged trees at the water's edge, where it waits for its prey to swim within catching distance. The second smallest heron in Canada, its plumage looks more bluish than green on its upper parts. In the breeding season, the yellow legs of the male turn to orange.

The rare Trumpeter Swan was once close to extinction, but now, thanks to successful measures taken to reintroduce it to its former breeding areas, the population is slowly increasing. Named for its call, a deep trumpet-like sound, this is one of the region's largest swans.

The Mute Swan is an introduced species from Europe which has become wild in a few parts of Canada.

The Canada Goose is **the** wild goose of the country. Most people see it on its spring or autumn migration to and from its breeding grounds. Its nest is a depression in the ground lined with sticks and dried stems, with an inner lining of down. The young hatch out after twenty-eight to thirty-three days.

Though common throughout the country, Canada Geese seem to prefer to nest in the muskeg region of the Hudson Bay lowlands, a largely waterlogged plain. Despite the similarity of all their markings, at least ten distinct subspecies of Canada Goose occur.

A pair of Canada Geese with that year's young are inseparable. The female leads the way, followed by the young, and the gander will bring up the rear. The young fly south with their parents in the fall and do not separate from them until they return to the nesting grounds the following spring.

and Queen Charlotte. The American Bittern is another widespread member of the family. It is a bird of fresh and saltwater marshes, swamps and wet thickets, often relying on its cryptic brown, buff and yellow plumage for concealment. The populations of both these birds contract southwards in the autumn, although a small percentage remains to winter north of the United States. The Great or Common Egret, the Black-crowned Night-Heron, the Green-backed Heron and the Least Bittern also breed, but are solely summer visitors. Other family members, such as the Snowy Egret, are irregular in their appearance as spring overshoots from the U.S.A. During the last few decades North America has been colonized by an Old World heron – the Cattle Egret. This was first recorded in South America in 1880, having probably crossed the Atlantic from West Africa, but it was not until the 1930s that the species expanded from its bridgehead in the Guianas. By the late 1940s and early 1950s, there had been a few sightings in the United States, but at the time it was thought that these might have been escapees from zoos or other collections. Then, in April 1952, one was found feeding around the feet of cattle on a farm in Massachusetts. The following day it was shot to establish the first record for the United States – what a pitiful end for an unusual bird! However, that lone Cattle Egret was just the tip of the iceberg, for during 1952 others turned up

in Illinois and Florida, as well as the first Canadian record. In late October, a juvenile appeared on a trawler working the Grand Banks off Newfoundland. It didn't survive, but others came north and in 1962 the first breeding record came from Ontario. The Cattle Egret has come a long way from Africa.

The largest Canadian freshwater bird is the American White Pelican, which breeds on suitable lakes from southern British Columbia to western Ontario. With its white plumage, black primary and secondary wing feathers and massive bill it is unmistakable, and, as every child knows, "His beak holds more than his belican." The Brown Pelican is the other North American species, but it is only a casual visitor.

Wildfowl are perhaps associated with freshwater more than any other family of birds; they do have webbed feed, but do not all say "quack!" They range in size from the huge Trumpeter Swan at one end of the scale to the Bufflehead at the other end. The family is split into three major subdivisions – swans, geese and ducks. There are two species of swan, with the Trumpeter being somewhat larger than the Tundra Swan. The latter, as its name suggests, is an Arctic breeding species; the subspecies with more yellow on its bill that occurs in Eurasia is known as Bewick's Swan. However the records committee in Britain is currently reviewing the specific identity of

Breeding throughout almost all of Canada, the Canada Goose varies greatly in size depending on the subspecies, but all of them show the distinctive black head and neck with the white throat and cheek patches that form a throat strap. The sexes are similar in appearance and breed adjacent to lakes, streams and marshes.

Migrating Canada Geese.

A female Mallard keeps watch while her ducklings rest. A common duck, the Mallard breeds mainly in western Canada and is found almost anywhere associated with freshwater ponds, lakes, marshes and flood water; it is sometimes even seen on the coast in winter. The Mallard feeds by upending itself in the water, paddling its feet to keep upright, with just its rear end visible above the surface. The orange and black bill of the female distinguishes it from similar species.

The beautifully marked male Harlequin Duck frequents rocky shorelines in summer, preferring heavy surf to tranquil beaches, while choosing to winter and breed inland on rivers and streams. Surprisingly, given its conspicuous white flashes and stripes, the male can look very dark at a distance. The species can sometimes be seen perched on rocks in midstream, but is generally rather shy.

The prominent crest of the male Hooded Merganser, which is an uncommon diving duck of wooded lakes and streams.

A pair of Red-breasted Mergansers. These are common diving ducks, especially along the coast in winter.

A young Osprey nearly ready to leave the nest. Ospreys are uncommon birds which feed only on fish, and are thus found chiefly on the coast, or near lakes and rivers.

this pair and it is possible that they might split the races into two species. Formerly the Trumpeter Swan was more widespread, but, due largely to hunting pressures, it has become endangered and now occurs only locally in western Canada. A third species, the Mute Swan, has become established in some parts of southern Canada. This species is native to Eurasia, where for centuries it has graced ornamental lakes and parks. For this reason it was brought to Canada, and subsequently some birds eventually established feral populations.

Of the geese, the most familiar are the Canada and Snow geese, the latter breeding in the Arctic together with the Brant, Greater White-fronted and Ross' geese. Some races of the Canada Goose also breed in the Arctic, but these are smaller than the more familiar interior races – sometimes as small as a mallard. To many this is the Canadian "honker" that personifies the wild goose, especially when, each spring and autumn, these birds migrate in arrow-shaped skeins along traditional flyways: their atmospheric honking flight calls as they pass overhead signify the changing seasons.

The most familiar duck is the mallard, a bird that is more common in the west of Canada than in the east, although, over recent years, there has been a marked increase in the eastern population. It is one of several ducks known as "dabbling ducks." When feeding these are birds of the shallow water around the margins of lakes, ponds and rivers, although they may roost in the relative security of deeper water. They feed from the surface of the water or gather food from the bottom by "upending." They are rapid fliers and rise quickly from the surface on takeoff. Close relatives include teals, wigeon, the Northern Pintail and the Northern Shoveler. Another group of ducks are the diving ducks, represented in temperate fresh waters by scaups, the Ring-necked Duck, the Redhead, the Canvasback, the Common Goldeneye and the Bufflehead.

Diving ducks are birds of deeper water than dabbling ducks, for, as their name implies, they dive for food. They are often heavier birds and need a runway of clear water for takeoff, pattering over the surface to gain momentum. Two species that have a divided distribution in Canada are the Harlequin Duck and Barrow's Goldeneye. The Harlequin Duck is a bird of fast-flowing rivers during the breeding season and wave-dashed coasts in winter. It occurs from the Rockies westward and in the east from Baffin Island south to the Gulf of St. Lawrence. Barrow's Goldeneye is also western oriented with only a small population in Labrador. These two species breed in Iceland, where, together with the Common Loon and the Red Phalarope, they are the only essentially Nearctic birds to breed regularly in the Western Palearctic.

The Osprey is a spectacular bird of prey that builds its nest in tall trees near water. At long distances, it can be identified by the characteristic crook in its long wings.

Close to, the Osprey is identified by its dark-brown upperparts, white underparts and white head with a dark stripe through the eye. The bird in the photograph is almost certainly male, as females tend to have some dark streaking on the breast, forming a necklace. The Osprey's deeply-hooked bill is ideal for tearing at its prey, which includes both sea and freshwater fish.

Franklin's Gull is a small, black-headed, red-billed gull that breeds on prairie lakes or marshes and feeds in flocks in fields.

Mergansers are specialized fish-eating ducks known as "sawbills" from the serrated-edged bill that has evolved to help hold the fish once captured. These birds occur across the country; Common and Hooded mergansers are mainly freshwater birds, both in the breeding season and in winter, while the Red-breasted Merganser is equally at home in the sea.

The most highly developed freshwater predator is the Osprey, a bird found throughout much of the world, but one that, because it is at the top of its food chain, is vulnerable to the cumulative effects of pollution. It is a wonderful bird to watch as it beats slowly over a lake or river watching for the slightest movement of a fish in the waters below. It may then hover over its intended victim before closing its wings and swooping down. The Osprey enters the water feet first in a cloud of spray, and emerges with a struggling fish as it beats its powerful wings to become airborne again. Moments later, before gaining any height, the Osprey shakes the water from its plumage and manoeuvres the fish so it is carried, head first, along the line of the body – an incredible act to watch.

Another family of freshwater birds are the rails, whose most familiar members are the American Coot and the Common Moorhen, although the latter is a localized summer resident with only a limited breeding range from Ontario to New Brunswick. These two mainly black aquatic birds spend much of their

A floating mat of vegetation provides a nesting site for a pair of Forster's Terns. Breeding in central southern Canada, these birds migrate south in winter. Though very similar to both Arctic and Common terns, their black-tipped bill distinguishes them from the Arctic Tern, while their grey tail, with its white outer edge, distinguishes them from the Common Tern.

Named for its ringing, vibrant call, the elegant and dignified Whooping Crane was becoming dangerously close to extinction and so is now carefully protected.

time in the water, feeding on aquatic vegetation and small animal life. The other members of the family are usually less conspicuous, being secretive birds of marshes and swamps where they creep silently through the protective screen of marsh plants. Four species breed in Canada, namely the Sora, Virginia, Yellow and King rails. The most widespread species is the Sora Rail, which is found in marshes from New Brunswick to British Columbia, while the Virginia Rail mainly occurs east of the Rockies. The diminutive Yellow Rail only occurs east of the mountains while the King Rail, the largest of the quartet, only breeds in southern Ontario. All four are summer visitors, the winter freeze separating the birds from their food of small aquatic animals and invertebrates.

One freshwater shore bird is Wilson's Phalarope, which occurs on sloughs and around the reedy margins of lakes and ponds south of the Arctic Circle, scarcely overlapping the range of the smaller Red-necked and Red phalaropes. It does not swim as much as its northern cousins, neither does it spend the winter months at sea, but rather, for the most part, on freshwater lakes in South America.

In their adult plumage, the gulls that occur in inland Canada have white bodies and grey wings; some also have black hoods. Bonaparte's Gull is a small, black-hooded species that breeds by ponds, lakes and muskegs to the west of James Bay, at the

southern end of Hudson Bay. It occurs throughout the broad belt of coniferous forest, for, unlike most other members of its family, it nests in trees! By contrast, the larger Franklin's Gull is a breeding bird of the prairie lakes and sloughs. The Laughing Gull, another North American black-hooded gull, formerly bred here, but was never common as southern Canada was at the extreme northern edge of the species' range. On the plus side has been the arrival of two European gulls as colonists in eastern Canada – the Common Black-headed Gull and the Little Gull. The latter is established at several sites and, like its local cousins, has a black hood. Just to be awkward, the Common Black-headed Gull actually has a brown, not a black, head. It is larger than either the Little or Bonaparte's gulls and so far has not become as well established as the Little Gull. All the other inland gulls south of the Arctic have white heads, the most widespread being the Ring-billed and Herring gulls. In the west, the California Gull, like Franklin's, is a gull of the prairies, while the Mew Gull has a more extensive range. The latter is more slightly built than the Ring-billed Gull, with a plain yellow-green bill and a dark eye. In Britain, it is known as the Common Gull, although this name is not strictly accurate, for it is only a winter visitor over much of England.

Terns are related to gulls and, in Canada, five species of tern breed by fresh water. Largest of these

The Spotted Sandpiper is found by rivers, streams, ponds, lakes and marshes, and is both common and widespread. When on the ground it constantly bobs its tail up and down, while in flight its wings are held stiffly bowed downwards, the wingbeats being very rapid but interspersed with occasional glides.

is the Caspian Tern, a localized breeder in scattered areas across Canada. This gull-sized tern has a strong orange/scarlet bill reminiscent of a carrot! The Common and Arctic terns are also birds of the coast, while Forster's Tern is mainly a bird of the marshes and rivers in south-central Canada. The small Black Tern is a more widespread species, found breeding in marshes and sloughs across the country south of the Arctic Circle.

Along with the geese, the Sandhill Crane is one of the more conspicuous migrants as it heads south to the United States from its Canadian breeding grounds. Sandhills are stately birds that breed in marshes, broad valleys, and on the tundra; they have been driven from the southern part of their range in Canada through loss of habitat to agriculture.

Pride of place must perhaps go to the Whooping Crane; larger than the mainly grey-brown Sandhill Crane, the adult is pure white with black primaries and red on the forehead and face. It has also suffered from loss of habitat, but, as it was never as widespread as the Sandhill, the population decline has driven it to the brink of extinction. It is one of the rarest North American birds and until it was discovered recently breeding in northern Alberta, all known breeding occurred in Wood Buffalo National

Park. The future of this bird is far from secure, for, as with all other cranes, the reproduction rate is low, added to which are the hazards of migration. Each autumn the Wood Buffalo birds fly south to winter at Aransas in Texas, returning north again in the spring. Much research by the Canadian Wildlife Service and their counterparts in the United States has been done into the breeding biology and population dynamics of Whooping Cranes; they lay two eggs, but as a rule only a single youngster fledges. In conjunction with the International Crane Foundation, a single egg is removed for use in two conservation projects. The first, the establishment of a captive flock by the Foundation, has been successful, and the information gathered has been applied to the conservation of the world's other endangered crane species. The second project involved placing eggs in the nests of Sandhill Cranes at Grays Lake National Wildlife Refuge in Idaho. The Grays Lake Sandhills pass the winter at Bosque del Apache in New Mexico, so the idea was to establish a second population of Whooping Cranes with a different wintering area. This was a great idea in theory, but in reality the results were very disappointing, as initial hopes were dashed when the success rate gradually declined. No eggs were taken from Wood Buffalo to Grays Lake in either 1989 or

Perched on a twig, a female Belted Kingfisher eyes the water below keenly as she waits for a fish to swim past.

Her prey successfully snatched from the water, the female Belted Kingfisher pauses before consuming it. The female is identified by its rusty-coloured flanks and belly band; the male of the species has only the blue breast band.

A resplendent male Yellow-headed Blackbird perches on a bullrush at the edge of a marsh. The white area on the wing of the male forms a noticeable patch in flight; females lack this patch and their plumage is dusky brown instead of black, with the head and breast usually being a buffish yellow.

Wintering in South America, the Lesser Yellowlegs is a common bird that migrates to Canada to breed. Two species of yellowlegs occur, the lesser and the greater. As its name implies, the lesser is the smaller of the two, and it also has a thinner, shorter, straight bill than the greater. The two species are often seen together on migration, and long, bright yellow legs are common to both. The Lesser Yellowlegs breeds in open woodlands and tundra near ponds and lakes.

A Willet in its winter plumage. A long-legged, long-billed wading bird, the Willet's summer plumage is browner and heavily mottled.

A pair of American Wigeon. The male is distinguished by his white forehead and cap, and a greenish patch from the eye to the nape, while the drabber female's head and neck has strong, dark streaking. Both sexes have bluish bills.

The colourful male Wood Duck, with its glossy green head and striking red eyes and bill, is a bird of woodland lakes and streams, as its name implies. It nests, not by the water's edge, but in holes or hollows in trees, and when their young hatch they climb to the entrance and drop to the ground.

The male Blue-winged Teal (right) is unmistakable, with a grey head and a conspicuous white crescent in front of the eye. The Green-winged Teal (far right) is Canada's smallest duck, measuring only twenty-seven centimetres in length.

1990; instead, the establishment of a second captive flock commenced. It would have been wonderful if the Grays Lake project had succeeded, for there can be fewer more exciting moments than seeing a Whooping Crane in the wild.

Pools and quiet bays along rivers and streams make ideal places for birds to drink and bathe, but some species have a way of life that is inexorably linked to running water. The Spotted Sandpiper is a shore bird, with distinctively spotted underparts in its nuptial plumage, that "teeters" over stones along the water's edge. It is also found around the stone margins of lakes, but outside the breeding season it can occur by other waters. It migrates south to winter as far away as Chile, although some do remain in southwestern British Columbia. Another species of the rocky streams and rivers is the American Dipper. This is a dumpy grey-brown bird of the mountainous west, which looks like a large wren with a weight problem! It feeds by diving beneath the surface of the

stream for small invertebrates and remains close to its home range throughout the year, only moving downstream when forced to do so in hard weather. The Belted Kingfisher is the only member of its family to be found north of Texas and it occurs widely in a variety of freshwater habitats from Newfoundland to British Columbia.

In the marshes one finds two species of breeding blackbird, the males of which are rather striking birds. The larger of the two is the Yellow-headed Blackbird, which occurs in the central and western parts of the country. The male has a chrome-yellow head and white wing patches. The Red-winged Blackbird is slightly smaller, a little slimmer and all black, except for red and yellow epaulettes on its "shoulders." It has a wider distribution than its yellow-headed relative, being found coast to coast. This is also the habitat where the Common Snipe breeds but, as marsh becomes wet meadow, so the transition to other open country and lowland habitats becomes apparent.

The male Greater Scaup (right). Far right: a coot feeding its young.

The peculiar lobed toes of the American Coot not only help to distinguish this bird from similar gallinules, but also help it to swim more effectively. An American Coot is anyway easy to identify by its heavy white bill with a dark band near the tip, the reddish shield on its forehead, and the white feathers on its undertail.

American Avocets are found on the shores of marshes and lakes in central southern Canada, where they breed in colonies.

A long, thin, slightly upturned bill identifies the American Avocet, whose plumage is mainly black and white with a rust-coloured head and neck. The long, blue legs facilitate wading in shallow water, where it searches for food by sweeping its bill from side to side in the water.

A long-legged, long-billed bird of marshes and swamps, the American Bittern is common but extremely difficult to observe, due to its habit of skulking amongst vegetation. The thin black streak on its neck distinguishes it from all other herons. Its method of avoiding detection is equally distinctive: when in danger or alarmed, bitterns adopt an upright stance, their neck, head and bill pointed skywards as they remain completely motionless, a tactic which helps them to blend with their surroundings and thus camouflages them.

The Northern Pintail is a widespread water bird. The male is distinguished from the female by his chocolate brown head, white neck and long, central tail feathers, the female having buff-brown feathers streaked with black.

A Double-crested Cormorant displaying at the nest clearly shows the bare, orange-coloured skin around the eye and on the throat patch which helps in its identification.

Lowlands and Open Country

It is perhaps in the lowlands and open spaces of Canada, as in many other developed countries, that the influence of man has had its greatest effect. It is here, where the ground has been managed for agriculture and where towns and cities, together with railroads and highways, have spread, that nature is often the loser. Much has changed since the land was first claimed by European settlers: prairie has been lost to the plough; wetlands have been drained and woodland and scrub cleared.

The raptors of the open country include the Turkey Vulture, a widespread species in North and South America that reaches the northern limit of its range in southern Canada. It is a conspicuous bird when in flight, as it glides effortlessly in search of

Northern Harrier eggs and nestlings. This species is a common hawk of grasslands and marshes, where it shares its hunting grounds with the Rough-legged Hawk; it feeds mainly on rodents.

Swainson's Hawk is found in the dry, open country of the west, where it hunts mainly prairie dogs and gophers, also eating large insects such as grasshoppers.

A Red-tailed Hawk mantling its prey. The Red-tailed Hawk is a lazy hunter, rarely hovering but rather perching on poles or treetops, where it is a well-known sight

food. As with other vultures, it is a carrion eater and has learned to benefit from the carcasses of mammals and other animals killed on the roads. Unlike other members of its family, the Turkey Vulture has ultra-sensitive olfactory organs and detects most of its food by smell. In areas of open grassland and around fresh- and saltwater marshes lives the Northern Harrier, a long-winged and long-tailed hawk. Formerly known as the Marsh Hawk, it occurs widely in the higher latitudes of the northern hemisphere; the change of name indicates its relationship with harriers in other parts of the world. The broad-winged hawks or buteos of the open country are the Ferruginous and Swainson's hawks, both of which are summer visitors. They found mainly in central-southern Canada, although Swainson's also has outlying populations in British Columbia and in the Yukon. The most widespread of this group of raptors is the Red-tailed Hawk, a bird familiar to those aware of birds of prey perching on roadside telegraph poles. It is a bird of both open country and woodland that chooses to nest on cliffs if trees are not available.

The falcons are swift-flying raptors of which the larger species – the Peregrine and Prairie falcons – breed on cliffs. The Prairie Falcon is restricted to the southwestern provinces, whilst the Peregrine, the most cosmopolitan falcon, ranges from coast to coast in Canada. It breeds on sea cliffs and, besides inland

A Prairie Falcon on the lookout for prey.

A male Greater Prairie-Chicken performs its courtship display. With tail cocked and crest erect, it bows and inflates its orange neck sacs behind its long, fanned, neck feathers. During this display the male makes its deep, hollow-sounding 'oo-loo-woo' call, known as booming, in front of the females on a defined courtship ground.

The Long-billed Curlew is the largest shore bird in Canada, and is easily distinguished by its slender, extremely long, down-curved bill and cinnamon-coloured upperparts. During the breeding season, it nests in meadows and pastures; the sexes are similar in appearance.

cliffs and crags, it has started to utilize skyscrapers, which must look like artificial cliffs! As far as the bird-hunting Peregrine Falcon is concerned, the attraction of cities is the abundance of feral pigeons that now populate parks and squares. The Peregrine, in spite of its love for pigeons, used to be called the Duck Hawk, recalling its superb mastery of the air in pursuit of wildfowl. The small falcons, the American Kestrel and the Merlin, occur in a variety of habitats and were formerly called the Sparrow Hawk and the Pigeon Hawk respectively.

The lowlands and open country are home to several species of game bird. Of the North American quails, the Mountain Quail is native to British Columbia and the Northern Bobwhite occurs in southern Ontario. The California Quail has been successfully established in southern Vancouver Island and the nearby mainland. Three other introductions have been the Gray Partridge, the

A Long-billed Curlew chick.

The largest of the godwits, the Marbled Godwit is brown in colour, its plumage being mottled above and, during breeding, barred below. Its long bill is usually slightly upturned, but can be straight, and it breeds in grassy meadows and on the edges of lakes in central Canada.

A Killdeer lowers itself over its four eggs, laid in a shallow scrape. This bird will feign personal injury to distract intruders away from its nest, and is identified by a double black breast band.

Chukar and the Ring-necked Pheasant from Eurasia, but naturally the prairies and open grasslands are home to the Sage Grouse, the Sharp-tailed Grouse and the Greater Prairie-Chicken. The Sage Grouse is a bird of the sagebrush, but its population has been so reduced through hunting that it is now extinct in British Columbia and has only a foothold in southeastern Alberta and southwestern Saskatchewan. The Greater Prairie-Chicken is a bird of the prairies and occurs mainly in southern Alberta, Saskatchewan and Manitoba. The Sharp-tailed Grouse is the most widespread of the three species, ranging from Quebec to the Alaskan border.

The natural open grasslands are, surprisingly, home to several species of shore birds such as the Long-billed Curlew, Marbled Godwit and Upland Sandpiper. All three breed in the grasslands but leave for other areas afterward. The curlew and the godwit are to be found along tidal shores during the winter, while the Upland Sandpiper migrates to the pampas of South America. On its breeding ground it can be almost as secretive as a rail among natural meadows, a habitat that it may share in part of its range with the striking black, white and yellow Bobolink. Only the male Bobolink has this smart plumage, and then just during the breeding season; for the remainder of the year he has a buff and black striated plumage like the female. In the autumn, the Bobolink heads south to winter in South America as far south as northern Argentina.

In the short-grass prairie breeds the Mountain Plover, a summer visitor to south-central Canada,

A Killdeer on its nest.

91

The Barn Swallow could be mistaken for the Cliff Swallow, as both species have bright cinnamon underparts and a red forehead and throat. However, the long streamers of its deeply-forked tail conclusively identify the Barn Swallow. It is a strong and elegant flier, common near farms, and it nests in farm buildings, under bridges and in caves.

although the majority of the population breeds in the short-grass prairie of United States. The Upland Sandpiper is another shore bird found in the grasslands of Canada, mainly west of the Great Lakes. Unlike the Mountain Plover, which winters in the United States, the Upland Sandpiper migrates to winter in the pampas of South America.

Another shore bird of open country is the Killdeer, a striking bird with a double black breast band and a rufous rump. It is related to the slightly smaller, ringed plovers and breeds over much of Canada south of Hudson Bay, mostly retreating south of the border before the onset of winter. It breeds in areas of disturbed ground and is therefore an obvious beneficiary of agriculture. At other times of the year, it is more a bird of the damp margins of ponds and marshes.

The majority of owls are woodland birds, but the rare Barn Owl and the widespread Short-eared Owl are birds of open country. The Barn Owl is confined to southwestern British Columbia and southern Ontario as a breeding species. It is a beneficial species on agricultural land as it preys on small rodents. In winter individuals wander farther afield and may be seen hunting during the day in hard weather. The Short-eared Owl is a bird of rough grassland and marshes, and has a wider distribution, being found over much of Canada during the breeding season. It is

a darker coloured bird than the Barn Owl and can be seen hunting during the day in the breeding season as well as during the winter. Both these owls have a really relaxed style of flight and flop around on silent wings like overgrown moths. The other owl of open country is the Burrowing Owl. A small, long-legged owl of the short-grass prairies, it is often associated with the burrows of rodents, who unwittingly provide it with suitable nest sites.

As breeding birds return from South America each spring, the Barn Swallow is a welcome sight. It is a widespread species that, before European settlers appeared on the scene, built mud and straw nests under cliff ledges or in caves, but now uses houses, barns and, more recently, concrete bridges as artificial substitutes. The Cliff Swallow has also made the switch from rock to concrete; like all the other members of the family, it is a summer visitor from the south. Not all species construct these nests; along earthen and sand river banks, the Northern Rough-winged and the Bank swallows excavate burrows in which they lay their eggs and rear their young.

Man has had a profound effect on the lowlands and open spaces of Canada and much has changed since European settlers tamed the land: ploughing the prairie, draining wetlands and clearing woodland and scrub. With the arrival of modern civilization several species have been introduced to Canada, some more successfully than others. The three most widespread species need no introduction, for they are the Feral Pigeon, the Common Starling and the House Sparrow – all found in association with agriculture and human habitation. Apart from being reminders of Europe, they have nothing to commend them; often they are agricultural pests or urban nuisances. In the wild, starlings and House Sparrows have usurped the nest sites of indigenous species such as Cliff and Tree swallows, and in comparatively few generations they have spread from coast to coast. Two other species, the Crested Myna and the Eurasian Skylark, that were introduced to Vancouver Island have not been as successful, and have not as yet crossed to the mainland. Introduced from Asia in the 1890s, the Crested Myna is a relative of the starling; elsewhere in the world introduced mynas have become pests, so, as far as Canada is concerned, it is a blessing that it has spread no further. The skylark, a bird of open grasslands and fields, is a renowned songster with a beautiful song that is delivered as the bird circles high above its breeding territory. Of all the introduced species, the skylark has had the least effect on the ecology of its new environment. It is not an opportunistic colonist and is therefore more vulnerable to hard winters and habitat changes than the other species. The only lark native to Canada is

the Horned Lark, which occurs in open habitats over much of the country from the Arctic to the short-grass prairies and from Newfoundland to British Columbia.

The House Sparrow from the Old World is a weaver and is unrelated to the New World sparrows. Some of those found in the lowlands and open country are, as is sometimes the case with birds of open habitats, fairly nondescript. Birds such as Cassin's and Brewer's sparrows are hardly likely to set the world alight! Sprague's Pipit is another small brown bird; the same cannot be said about the Western Meadowlark and two more longspurs – the Chestnut-collared and McCown's. All three are smart, well-marked birds that even a non-birder would probably notice. In years gone by the Brown-headed Cowbird, which now occurs across the breadth of Canada, followed the buffalo herds, feeding on the insects disturbed by the feet of the great beasts. Times have changed, and the buffalo no longer exist in their former numbers, so the resourceful birds have turned to cattle and their range has extended accordingly. When this happens, someone has to suffer, and, in this case, it is the small insectivorous and seed-eating birds. For, like the cuckoo of Britain and Europe, the cowbird is parasitic and lays its eggs in other birds' nests – all the pleasure and none of the hard work!

The heavy bill of the White-crowned Sparrow is ideal for crushing the seeds which form a major part of its diet. Interestingly, the young are fed solely on insects at first.

In the breeding season, the Chipping Sparrow is identified by its bright chestnut crown, white eyebrows and grey nape and cheek. The female builds the nest with fine grass, usually in a tree in open woodland, and lines it with hair, incubating three to five eggs; the species is common throughout most of Canada.

A bright reddish-orange rump and tail identify the Fox Sparrow in eastern Canada. However, the plumage is highly variable and in the west these birds are much darker and drabber.

The distinctive head pattern of the adult Lark Sparrow helps to identify it accurately.

The Song Sparrow builds its nest on the ground, breeding in bushy thickets and shrubbery close to ponds and streams. The adults are highly variable in size and plumage, but all show a greyish line above the eye.

As he sings to proclaim his territory, the male Red-winged Blackbird shows off his yellow-bordered, bright-red wing patches.

The male Brewer's Blackbird is distinguished from the female by its yellow eye and glossy black plumage with a purplish sheen; the female has a brown eye and brown-grey plumage. A bird that often breeds in loose colonies, this blackbird's nest is constructed of twigs and grasses mixed with mud and lined with fine grass or hair. The nest is usually found in a tree or shrub, but it can be on the ground, and is nearly always built near water.

The black body and bright yellow head and breast of the male Yellow-headed Blackbird make it unmistakable. Though it favours freshwater marshes and reedy lakes, this bird can also be seen foraging for food in grain fields in southwest Canada.

A splendid male Indigo Bunting, bill agape, rests in the grass. Common in hedgerows and wood margins, this bird has a long and varied song which is most audible around midday.

The Lazuli Bunting is found in bushy scrub and open woodland, especially near water, throughout southwestern Canada.

The familiar Black-capped Chickadee needs no introduction. Common in most areas of Canada, it is one of the most frequent visitors to the suburban garden if food is provided.

The Chukar (right) is an Asian bird that has been introduced into Canada. Far right: Bewick's Wren, which can be distinguished from other wrens by its conspicuous eye stripe, white underparts and solid brown back.

The brightly-coloured male Purple Finch is the size of a sparrow, which bird the duller-coloured female and the immature Purple Finch resemble.

A female Yellow-shafted Flicker feeds its young at the entrance to its nest hole in a dead tree. The red patch on the nape of the neck helps to identify this species; in addition, the males have a black 'moustache', though otherwise the sexes are very similar in plumage. This particular woodpecker can often be seen on the ground, where it feeds on ants.

The Ruby-throated Hummingbird breeds across much of southern Canada, with the exception of the far west. The characteristic red throat is only present in the male.

Its bright-red plumage and bill make the male Cardinal almost unmistakable. Both sexes have a sizeable conical bill and pointed crests, while the male also has a distinctive black throat patch. This bird has greatly expanded its range northward, and is becoming more frequent in Canada.

The male American Goldfinch is commonly known as the 'wild canary'. Its bright yellow plumage is strikingly offset by a black cap, wings and tail. The male's wings have white bars and its rump is also white, while the female is much duller and lacks the black cap. This finch is found on roadsides, in orchards and in weedy fields, and it is especially fond of thistle seeds, which gives it yet another name: the 'thistle bird'.

Large and plump, with a stubby bill, the Pine Grosbeak is usually very tame. Its reddish plumage and double wing bars help to identify the male, while the female is greyish overall, with olive on the head and rump, though it too has the distinctive double wing bars. These are birds of the coniferous forests in summer, but they can be found in deciduous woodland, apple orchards and suburban shade trees in winter.

Both sexes of the Mourning Dove incubate the eggs – the male during the day, and the female at night.

The American Crow is the largest of the crows, but is smaller than the raven, and its long, black bill is also much less heavy than the raven's. All black and glossy feathered, it is best identified by its call, the well-known 'caw'.

A California Quail.

A male Yellow Warbler feeding its nestlings. Rusty-red streaking on the underparts help to identify this bird, whose nest is usually built in a fork of twigs in a shrub or a tree and is made of fine grasses, lined with cotton and plant down. The young leave the nest nine to twelve days after hatching.

A rich, fruity, bubbling song distinguishes the Western Meadowlark from its look-alike, the Eastern Meadowlark, both of which occur in Canada. Its main plumage features in summer are a yellow throat, breast and belly, a black, V-shaped necklace on the throat, black streaking on the flanks, and a striped head. The call is very distinctive: a throaty 'chuck'. Found in open, grassy stubble fields in autumn, this bird prefers drier habitats than the Eastern Meadowlark.

A member of the flycatcher species, the Eastern Kingbird is most often seen perched in the open on a tree or post, where it waits to fly out and catch passing insects. These birds are identified by their dark, almost black, upperparts, white underparts and the white terminal band on their tail.

A Ring-necked Pheasant is a strikingly plumaged species that has been introduced into Canada from Europe and Asia.

Perhaps the commonest and certainly the smallest woodpecker in Canada, the Downy Woodpecker is the one most likely to visit a garden feeding station. For a woodpecker, it has an extremely short, slender bill, and this, together with its size, distinguishes it from the similarly marked Hairy Woodpecker that occupies the same habitat.

Unmistakable when seen properly, the Red-headed Woodpecker is the only woodpecker with a red head, neck and throat combined with a black necklace and white underparts. It nests in holes in dead trees.

Common on tundra, marshland and in fields, the Sandhill Crane is grey in colour, though its plumage may become reddish brown when residues in the mud, often present on the bill, stain the crane's feathers during preening. It has a distinctive, reddish patch of bare skin on the forehead that aids identification. Cranes are easily distinguished from herons in flight as they fly with necks outstretched, whilst herons fold their necks, and on the ground cranes are distinctive because their feathers droop over the rump, forming a 'bustle'. After breeding has finished they usually migrate south in large flocks.

Screech Owls, whose ear tufts and yellow eyes make good identifying marks. Two different colour forms, or phases, occur in the east of the country and the Eastern Screech-Owl, as it is known, can be either red or grey.

Although its markings and ear tufts are similar to those of the Long-eared Owl, the Great Horned Owl is much larger. Several colour forms occur in this species, ranging from dark brown through reddish-brown to extremely pale, greyish-brown plumages. As with all owls, these birds swallow their prey whole, later coughing up pellets of bone, fur, feathers and other indigestible matter.

The Screech Owl is found in a variety of habitats, from orchards, parks, and gardens to open woodland and swamps. This owl is purely nocturnal and is most easily located by its call, a long, quavering whistle which may descend in pitch towards the end. It nests in holes in trees.

Despite its enormous beak, the Bald Eagle is more of a scavenger than an active hunter; its food consists mainly of dead fish washed up either along the coast or by lakes and rivers. Recently the Bald Eagle has been declining in numbers.

Most adult Red-tailed Hawks are identified by their broad, reddish tails, which are darker red above than below. However, there are several different colour forms of this hawk in Canada, in some of which the red is very pale, or even non-existent. The bird is common in open country.

Coasts and Seashore

The shores and coastlines of Canada are washed by all three oceans of the northern hemisphere: the Arctic, the Atlantic, and the Pacific. This means that there is a wealth of sea birds on the birdlists, although it is in the Atlantic and the Pacific oceans that the widest variety of pelagic species can be found.

Some of the greatest oceanic travellers are the "tubenoses"; this family includes the albatrosses, the shearwaters and the petrels. They are birds found throughout the oceans of the world, and are often best known to sailors and fishermen. Only a handful of species breed in Canada, choosing remote, isolated rat-free sites on cliffs and islands. Other species are only seen off the coast as they pass by on their annual migrations, or perhaps when "wrecked" after a storm.

In eastern Canada the Northern Fulmar, Manx Shearwater and Leach's Storm-Petrel breed. The Northern Fulmar is a grey and white bird that glides effortlessly on stiff wings, using the updrafts and eddies that blow along the cliffs where it breeds. It was only in 1977 that the Manx Shearwater was first discovered breeding in Newfoundland, while the smaller Leach's Storm-Petrel breeds in colonies along both the Atlantic and the Pacific coasts. The only other breeding tubenose is the Fork-tailed Storm-Petrel found along the coasts of British Columbia.

Non-breeding shearwaters, in the form of the Greater and Sooty shearwaters, appear off the coasts of Nova Scotia and Newfoundland during the summer months. Both these birds breed in the southern hemisphere; the Greater Shearwater breeds almost exclusively on islands of the Tristan da Cunha group in the South Atlantic. The Sooty Shearwater has a wider breeding distribution and in summer is also present off the coasts of British Columbia, together with several other species that visit the North Pacific from austral breeding grounds. Also present is Wilson's Storm-Petrel, considered by some authorities to be the world's most abundant bird, for it breeds in colonies that number millions on subantarctic islands, such as South Orkney.

The albatrosses are the largest members of the family and, although four species have been recorded in Canadian waters, only the dark-plumaged Black-footed Albatross appears annually during the summer along the Pacific coast.

The largest breeding sea bird in the North Atlantic is the immaculate Northern Gannet; it is pure white with a cream head and black wing-tips, although juveniles are dusky, becoming increasingly white as they mature. Gannets breed on several islands off the southeast coast of Quebec, the best known of which is Bonaventure Island. It is their spectacular performance as fishermen in coastal waters that often attracts attention. Beating slowly over the sea, sometimes as much as a hundred feet above the surface, they watch for the glint of an unsuspecting fish before closing their wings and plunging after their prey; only at the last possible moment before entering the water are the wings thrust backward along the line of the body.

Another large fish-eating sea bird is the Great Cormorant, which is also restricted to the Atlantic coasts, where it occurs together with the Double-crested Cormorant; the latter is a slightly smaller species also found along the British Columbian coast and on inland lakes and rivers. Down the Pacific coast of North America are two other, purely maritime, species: the Brandt's and Pelagic cormorants.

Gulls are perhaps most people's idea of typical sea birds; in Canada the Herring and Great Black-backed gulls are found along the Atlantic coast, while the Glaucous, the Iceland and Thayer's gulls number among those breeding on Arctic coasts and islands, and the Glaucous-winged Gull is found in British Columbia, to whose shores both Heermann's and Western gulls are non-breeding visitors. The Herring Gull has a wider distribution as it is one of several species that nest by freshwater lakes and rivers. The larger gulls mentioned here are all opportunists who will exploit any available food source, be it a city garbage dump or the remains of a salmon left by a bear whose eyes were bigger than its stomach! They

The Herring Gull is a universal scavenger, which is not only found abundantly along the coast, but is also present around inland lakes, rivers, in fields, and especially at garbage dumps. Along the coast it can be seen either following fishing boats, picking up offal, or on the shore, where it picks up stranded fish and other animals, such as starfish. It is also partial to molluscs, which it drops from the air onto the beach in order to break them open.

A Herring Gull with its scavenged prey.

An Arctic Tern alights beside its young chick on a pebble-strewn, sandy shore. One to four eggs are usually laid and the immature gull is distinguished from the adult by its black bill.

Famous for its extraordinary migration, the Arctic Tern probably sees more daylight and travels further than any other animal. After breeding in the north, in almost perpetual daylight, this bird then migrates to spend the winter near the Antarctic, where it again enjoys very long hours of daylight.

A Double-crested Cormorant lowering over its chick has already lost the feature for which it is named. Early in the spring the adult has a tuft of feathers either side of the head which are whitish in Western Cormorants and black in Eastern Cormorants, but these are quickly lost once breeding commences. The nestling has a pink, rather than a yellow, throat patch.

follow fishing boats for the offal cast overboard as the catch is gutted and they rob Common Eiders and other diving birds for an easy meal.

Arctic and Common terns are summer visitors to the coasts, although both occur inland. While feeding their young they are targets for passing jaegers, who force them, with great agility, to drop the fish the terns are carrying. Jaegers, although Arctic breeders, pass along the coasts in spring and autumn to winter in the southern hemisphere. However no other form of life can match the Arctic Tern when it comes to travelling. This delicate bird breeds north of the Arctic Circle, as well as in northeastern Canada, and winters along the edges of the pack ice that rings the frozen wastes of Antarctica. A truly intercontinental commuter, it sees more daylight in any twelve-month period than any other form of life.

Along both the Atlantic and Pacific coasts, auks are to be found and fourteen of the twenty North American species have been recorded in Canada; some breed there, others are winter visitors, while yet others, including Xantus' Murrelet, only appear accidentally. Auks are small sea birds, usually dumpy, and with an upright stance caused their legs being set near the "stern." As a result they resemble mini-penguins; however, they are not related and auks are able to fly on their short stubby wings. Like the penguins they are supremely adapted to life at sea

and "fly through" the water to catch their prey of fish and other marine life. Within the family there is considerable variation in size, bill shape and head adornments of which the puffins are most characteristic. The Atlantic Puffin, which is found in Labrador, Newfoundland, Nova Scotia and southeastern Quebec, has a comical appearance with its black and white plumage and multi-coloured, parrot-like, triangular bill; in the past, this bird was actually known to mariners and fishermen as the "sea-parrot." In recent years the similar-looking Horned Puffin has been discovered breeding in British Columbia, where the third type, the Tufted Puffin, also breeds. This latter is a mainly black auk, with a red and yellow bill, a white face and wonderful yellow plumes that hang over the back of the head. The smallest species is the Dovekie or Little Auk and the largest living species are the Common and Thick-billed murres and the Razorbill, all of which are to be found along the Atlantic coasts.These are smaller than the now-extinct Great Auk, which was a flightless bird, like a giant Razorbill, that once bred on Funk Island, Newfoundland, and perhaps at other sites along the coast. At its breeding grounds it was easily killed as a source of fresh meat by sailors. By 1844 it was extinct, although there were subsequent unconfirmed reports of sightings from the Newfoundland Banks. Both the murres reach the

A pair of Cassin's Auklets, snug in their nesting site: a crevice under stones where only one egg is laid in a nest of plant material. Their plumage is all dark except for a whitish belly and a very small white crescent over the eye.

Found on the Atlantic coast and in the eastern Arctic, the strikingly coloured Black Guillemot is unlikely to be confused with any other species.

A pair of Red-breasted Mergansers, clearly demonstrating the difference in colour between the sexes: the brighter plumage belongs to the male.

Pacific; the Thick-billed, which breeds in Alaska, was also recently discovered breeding in British Columbia. The Common Murre has a more extensive distribution, breeding both in northeastern Canada and on islands off the coast of British Columbia. Both species wander farther afield in winter. The Black Guillemot of the North Atlantic has a counterpart in British Columbia in the very similar Pigeon Guillemot; both are black and white auks with scarlet legs and feet. Other Pacific auks do not have Atlantic counterparts; some, such as the Marbled and Ancient murrelets and Cassin's and Rhinoceros auklets, breed, while several others occur only as accidentals. During the summer of 1990, an Ancient Murrelet appeared off the west coast of Lundy, a granitic island off southwestern England, much to the delight and amazement of birders throughout the British Isles – a Pacific auk spotted off a lonely isle half a world away in another ocean is quite extraordinary. Not all these species nest along the coasts, for the Marbled Murrelet confounded sceptics when the first nests were found high in conifers!

During the winter months some sea birds leave their breeding sites for the open ocean, while others move to the sea from freshwater habitats. These species include the divers, grebes and some species of wildfowl. Bay ducks such as scaups, Redheads and Canvasbacks are found in estuaries and sheltered bays, where they are joined by the fish-eating Red-breasted Merganser. The Harlequin Duck leaves the mountain rivers for the turbulent waters off rocky coasts; the Oldsquaws, scoters and eiders, all mainly Arctic breeders, head south along the coasts to reach more hospitable waters in which to winter. The Common Eider breeds around the coasts of the Arctic and northeastern Canada; for centuries, the downy feathers from the female's breast have been collected in Iceland and Northern Europe and used for bedding – hence the bird's French name Eider à duvet. There are three other species of eider, of which the drake King Eider is the most beautiful. This species breeds in Arctic Canada, but occurs farther south in winter. Until the late nineteenth century, there was another sea duck that probably used to breed along the coast of Labrador – the aptly named Labrador Duck. It appears never to have been a common bird and, like other members of its family, it moved south down the coast during the winter months. The last known Canadian bird was shot in April 1871 in New Brunswick, although the species survived until 1878, when the last known bird was recorded in New York State. The Labrador Duck was so poorly documented that we do not know if it bred in the United States, although contemporary writers believed that it only bred in Labrador. If such is the case, the species probably did occur in Canadian waters between 1871

Inhabiting rocky shores, and breeding only on the extreme west coast of Canada, the Black Oystercatcher is immediately recognisable from its all-black plumage, long red bill and distinctive pink legs.

and 1878, but passed unrecorded.

A variety of shore birds are to be found along the rocky coasts, tidal mud flats and salt marshes, but comparatively few breed there. Among the breeding species is the Black Oystercatcher, a bird of rocky shores found in British Columbia, and a close relative of the American Oystercatcher, which is only a casual visitor from the United States. There is speculation that there may have been the occasional record of the European Oystercatcher from northeastern Canada. It is a very similar bird to the American species, but the upper-parts are much blacker and, unlike its transatlantic cousin, it has a long white wedge running up its back. The nearest breeding areas for the European species are Iceland, the Faeroes and the British Isles. During the winter, rocky shores in the east are home to the Purple Sandpiper, a bird who lives on wave-splashed rocks; its counterpart along the Pacific coast is the very similar and more appropriately named Rock Sandpiper. The western shores also provide winter feeding for the Surfbird, the Black Turnstone and the Wandering Tattler.

The Semipalmated Plover breeds across Canada on northern coasts as well as on gravel beds by fresh water. It has a close relative in the larger and bigger-billed Common Ringed Plover of the Old World. The latter has a toehold in Canada by breeding on Baffin, Devon and Ellesmere islands, but in the autumn these birds return to the Old World to winter. The paler Piping Plover has a more limited range, being confined to southern Canada from Alberta to Newfoundland.

The greatest variety of shore birds is to be found on the tidal flats of estuaries and inlets, where the tiny Least Sandpiper, an Arctic breeder, can be found alongside the stately Long-billed Curlew and the Marbled Godwit from the latters' breeding areas in the interior provinces. This confusion of species can survive alongside one another because of their different feeding requirements. The Least Sandpiper, for example, probes little more than the top centimetre of mud in search of food while the Long-billed Curlew has a bill that may be as much as 19 cms. long! Some shore birds probe the mud at random, but the two species of dowitcher, the Long- and the Short-billed, feed with such a rapid probing action that they look like sewing machines! The Ruddy Turnstone characteristically turns over stones, seaweed and other debris along the tideline in search of prey. It occurs on both the Atlantic and Pacific coasts, whereas the closely related Black Turnstone

A Black Oystercatcher, its red eye ring clearly visible, grasps a limpet.

The Purple Sandpiper is found all year round, on Canada's eastern seaboard; it favours rocky coasts when on migration, and in winter can frequently be seen on jetties. It prefers to breed on mossy tundra near the coast, but has been seen well inland. The slender and slightly decurved bill has an orange base and this, together the bird's short yellow legs, helps to identify it. The Purple Sandpiper is often very tame.

is restricted to the rocky parts of the west coast.

Shore birds can present an identification problem to novice birders and experts alike, for many species may differ in their breeding and non-breeding plumages, and in the appearance of adults and juveniles – fortunately most of the males and females are similar! If the novice concentrates on bill shape and length, wing bars, and tail patterns, then by process of elimination and with the help of a good field guide, the shore bird may be identified, or at least reduced to perhaps two or three possibilities. As with any unfamiliar bird, it is always advisable to make concise notes before referring to the books; one's memory can be unconsciously affected by the field guide!

Coasts are associated with relatively few land birds, most of which are associated with neighbouring habitats. Raptors such as the Bald Eagle, the Osprey and the Peregrine and Gyr falcons haunt coasts, attracted there by the fish and birdlife on which they prey. The mighty Bald Eagle is also a scavenger, clearing the remains of carcasses; it is commonest along the Pacific coast, scarcer in the east. The Bald Eagle also occurs across Canada and is found in a variety of habitats, never far from water. One might not expect a swift to be associated with coasts, but in British Columbia the Black Swift breeds along sea cliffs.

One last word about birding on coasts, and in fact anywhere in wide open spaces: take a telescope and tripod with you. The latest optics and the convenience of a robust, yet lightweight, tripod will open up a whole new world to anyone who has yet to try the experience. To scan the skyline for passing shearwaters or to be able to identify ducks on the far side of a lake, when previously they were merely black dots, is a whole new ball game! Good luck!

For further reading
Finlay J.C. (1984) *A Bird-Finding Guide to Canada* (Hurtig)
Godfrey, W. Earl (1986) *The Birds of Canada* (Revised edition) (National Museum of Science (Canada))
National Geographic Society (1987) *Field Guide to the Birds of North America*
Scotter, Ulrich and Jones (1990) *Birds of the Canadian Rockies* (Prairie)

Thick-billed Murres breed on ledges on rocky coastal cliffs mainly in the northeast. They breed in colonies, often together with Common Murres, and together may number many thousands. The short, thick bill has a narrow, white line at the base.

Nesting in large colonies on cliffs, Common Murres are distinguished from other alcids by their white sides and long, slender bills.